UNHIJACKED:
CAPTURE THE DAY

A Companion Journal to HIJACKED

A Simple Daily Practice to End
the Day Without Escaping

JIM KOETTING

UNHIJACKED: Capture the Day

Copyright © 2026 by Jim Koetting

This is a companion journal to *HIJACKED* by Jim Koetting

Book Cover Design by Brittany Becker
Interior Layout and Design by Brittany Becker

ISBN: 979-8-9942374-9-6

Published by:
CEOM Publishing
1228 W. 62nd Street, Kansas City, MO 64113
https://ceompublishing.com

CEOM | PUBLISHING

UNHIJACKED: CAPTURE THE DAY

CONTENTS

WELCOME 1

Welcome: What This Journal Is (and What It Isn't) 2

INTRODUCTION: WHY THIS JOURNAL WORKS 5

The Night Isn't the Problem. It's the Signal. 6

Why Writing Works When Willpower Fails 7

When You Can't Change the Day, You Can Change
What the Day Does to You 9

Clarity, Growth, and the Moment You Start to Return 10

THE PRACTICE: HOW TO CAPTURE THE DAY 13

How to Use This Journal (Or, How to Begin Without
Getting It "Right") 14

How to Use the Daily Pages (One Spread at a Time) 16

The Two Prompts (How This Journal Works) 18

15-Minute Reset (A Simple Daily Practice) 20

When You Miss a Day (How to Restart Without Shame) 22

JOURNAL PAGES 25

Left Page Supporting Questions 26

Right Page Supporting Questions 27

CLOSING 197

Reflections 198

Looking Back 199

Last Page 201

WELCOME

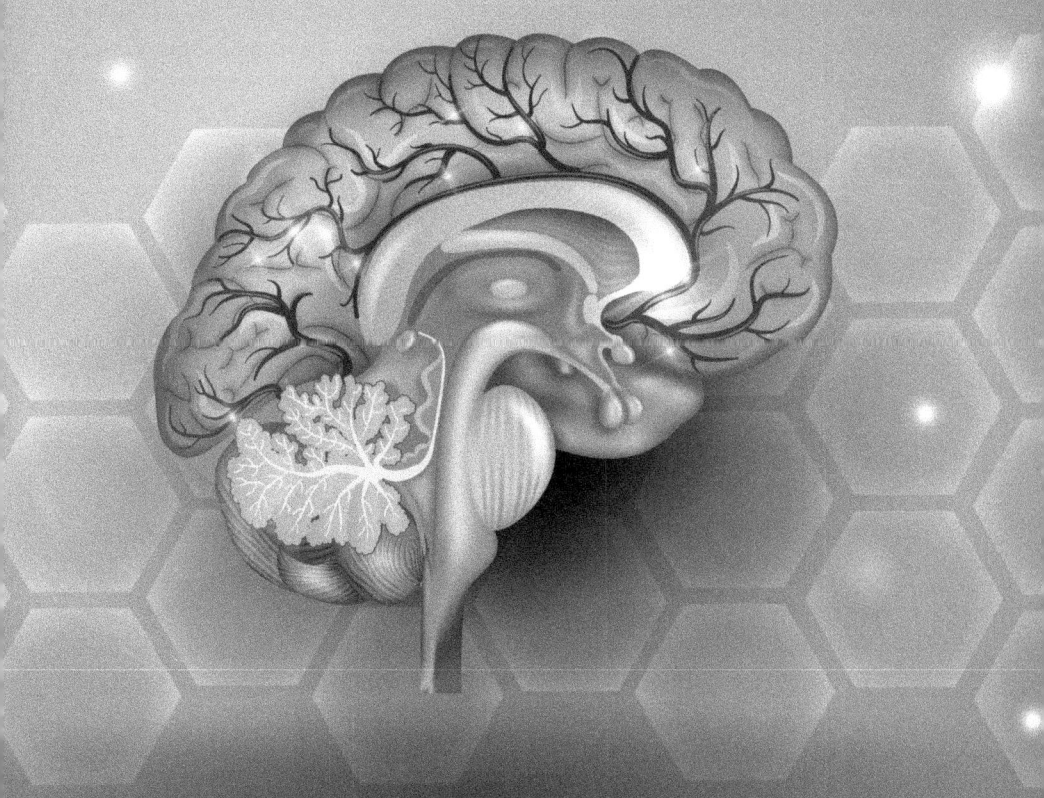

Welcome: What This Journal Is (and What It Isn't)

WELCOME.

If you're holding this journal, there's a good chance you've been living with a particular kind of exhaustion—one that isn't always visible to the people around you. It's the fatigue that comes from carrying too much stimulation, too much responsibility, too many unfinished thoughts, and too little space to process any of it.

This journal exists because most people don't need more information. They need a way to come back to themselves.

UNHIJACKED: Capture the Day is not meant to become another project on your list, another obligation you fail to keep up with, or another "self-improvement" item that quietly turns into a source of guilt. It is meant to be a small act of return at the end of your day—a simple place where the weight of the day can land so it doesn't have to follow you into your night.

It may help to say what this journal is not.

- It is not a diary meant to document every event.
- It is not a place to write beautifully.
- It is not therapy, and it does not require you to relive your pain.
- It is not a performance you have to get right.
- And it is not a tool designed for people with perfect habits.

It's for people who are tired.

It's for people who reach the end of the day and realize they've been running on adrenaline, obligation, distraction, and momentum—and they don't quite know how to turn it off without numbing out. It's for people who feel the pull of their phone at night and wonder why it seems harder and harder to be alone with their own thoughts. It's for people who have done the best they can today, and still feel like something inside them is unfinished.

This journal gives you something simple to do in that moment.

It gives you a place to write down the day.

Not because your day was dramatic. Not because your life is broken. But because your mind was never designed to carry unprocessed stress without an outlet. The modern world demands that you keep moving, keep responding, keep performing, and keep producing—and then it offers you an endless supply of distractions as your "recovery." But distraction is not recovery. It is a postponement.

This journal is an alternative.

It helps you complete the day.

If you use it the way it's designed, you will slowly begin to experience something many people haven't felt in a long time: evenings that belong to you again. Sleep that is less crowded. A mind that stands down more easily. A nervous system that feels less hunted.

You don't have to believe all of that yet. You only have to begin.

INTRODUCTION:
WHY THIS JOURNAL WORKS

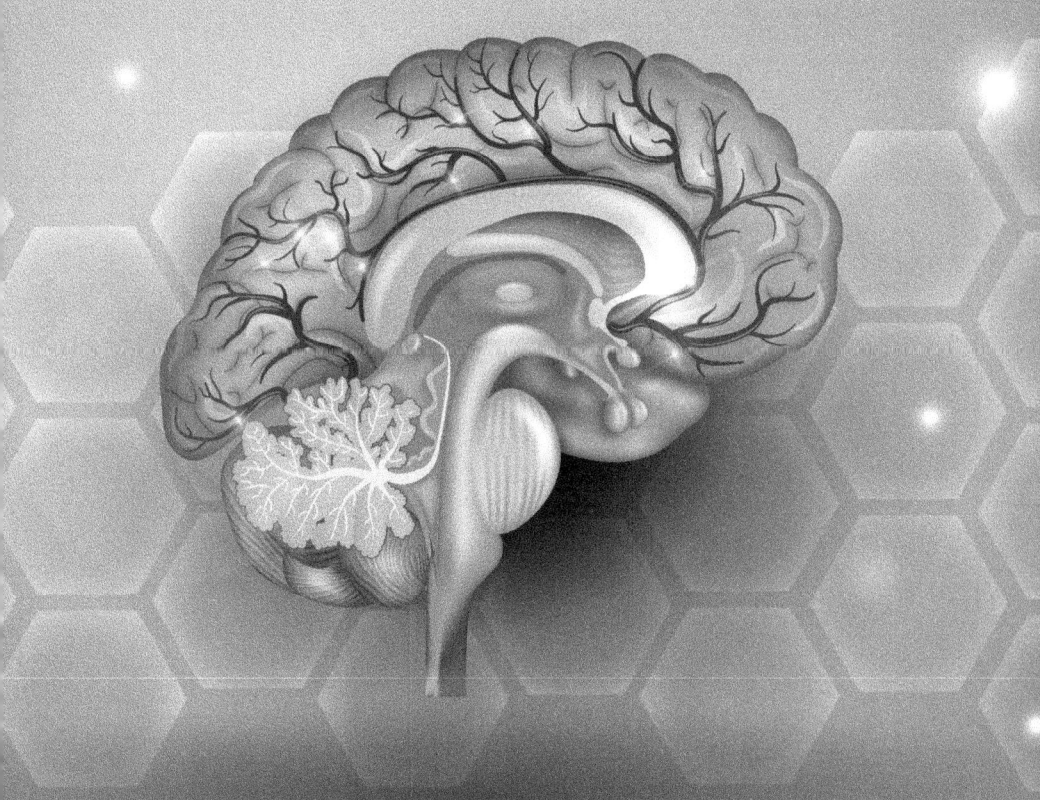

The Night Isn't the Problem.
It's the Signal.

There's a moment most people don't talk about. The day finally ends, the house gets quieter, the world stops asking for a few minutes, and you sit down "just to take a break." The phone is already nearby—often already in your hand. You may not even feel like you're choosing it. Your thumb knows what to do before your mind catches up. A quick check becomes a scroll. A scroll becomes a trance. The news, social media, videos, messages—anything that keeps your attention moving so your thoughts don't have to settle anywhere uncomfortable.

If the day was especially heavy, you might add a beer or a glass of wine—not as a celebration, but as a way to soften the edges. It's a familiar ritual, and in the short term it works. The mind quiets down. The pressure fades. Time disappears. Then, later—sometimes when the screen goes dark, sometimes as you lie in bed—something inside you notices the cost. The evening is gone again, and the rest you wanted never really arrived. You didn't recover; you simply checked out.

If this is your pattern, it isn't a sign of weakness. It's a sign of overload. Most people don't waste their nights because they lack discipline; they do it because they're trying to regulate a nervous system that's been carrying too much all day. When you're exhausted, your brain reaches for the fastest relief it can find, and modern life has produced an almost perfect off-switch: endless stimulation, easy distraction, and a steady drip of dopamine that asks nothing from you. The phone is not merely a habit. For many people, it has become their primary coping tool.

The problem is that checking out doesn't actually mark the day. It postpones it. It delays stress without releasing it, numbs emotion without processing it, and gives you a temporary escape at the price of unfinished weight. That weight doesn't vanish; it follows you into sleep, then shows up in the morning as fog, irritability, anxiety, or the dull sense that life is happening somewhere else. This journal isn't meant to shame you for coping. It's meant to offer you an alternative—something gentle, practical, and surprisingly effective: a way to complete the day instead of carrying it.

Why Writing Works
When Willpower Fails

Most people assume journaling is for people who love writing. They picture a calm person with a beautiful notebook, a clear mind, and the kind of life where feelings arrive in neat sentences. They imagine insight on demand, or a polished record they'll someday reread. And because they don't feel like that kind of person, they never start. But the form of journaling that helps the most isn't about writing well. It's about doing something your brain rarely gets to do anymore: slowing down long enough to notice what is actually happening inside you.

When thoughts stay trapped in the mind, they tend to multiply. They echo and distort and return at inconvenient times. Stress becomes background static. Irritation becomes a constant edge. Worry becomes a loop that runs while you're driving, brushing your teeth, or trying to fall asleep. Inside the head, everything is loud and slippery. On paper, the experience changes. What was swirling becomes visible. What was unnamed becomes specific. The mind begins to organize itself around what's true rather than what's loudest.

This is why journaling increases self-awareness over time. It doesn't magically make you wise; it simply makes your inner life observable. Patterns appear—triggers you didn't notice, beliefs you've been obeying, habits you've been repeating for years. You begin to see the same frustrations returning, the same disappointments, the same fears, the same resentments, and the same places where you abandon what you need. Once you can see the pattern, you stop confusing it for fate. You can't change what you can't see, and a journal is one of the simplest ways to start seeing clearly.

There's also a physiological reason writing helps. When people write honestly about emotional experience, the brain begins to move the experience out of the reactive, survival-driven mode and into the part of the mind that can make meaning and decisions. You don't need the scientific terms to recognize the effect. Sometimes you write a few true sentences and the body softens. Your shoulders drop. Your breathing changes. The problem isn't solved, but it becomes more manageable because you've stopped carrying it alone in the dark. Journaling acts like a pressure-release valve. It gives stress a place to go, which is one reason people who write consistently often sleep better and feel less emotionally over-loaded. The mind doesn't have to keep rehearsing the day if the day has been placed somewhere.

When You Can't Change the Day, You Can Change What the Day Does to You

There are days when the best you can say is that you made it through. Too many obligations, too much noise, too little margin, too little support. On those days people don't need more advice and they don't need a new system; they need relief. Journaling doesn't remove hard days, but it changes what hard days do to you. It reduces the tendency to carry them forward as tension, rumination, and quiet dread.

Research has repeatedly shown that brief periods of honest writing—often as little as fifteen or twenty minutes for several days—can lead to measurable improvements in mental and physical well-being. One of the simplest explanations is also the most humane: writing helps the mind organize emotional upheaval. When experience is chaotic and unnamed, it feels endless. When it is structured into language, it becomes finite. Not easy, not pleasant, but manageable. That shift alone can reduce anxiety and rumination, and it can give a person a sense of internal stability that no amount of scrolling can provide.

This organizing effect also improves decision-making. When thoughts stay inside your head, they're noisy and distorted. You react instead of choose. You assume instead of test. On paper you can separate facts from feelings and observe what you actually know versus what you fear. You can see the assumptions you've been obeying without realizing it. You can identify where you're stuck and why. A journal becomes a place where you stop being dragged by your mind and begin to lead it.

Over time, writing also strengthens emotional intelligence. It gives you a language for your internal life, which is often the missing piece in relationships. People don't become reactive because they are cruel; they become reactive because they can't name what's happening inside them. A journal teaches truth-telling without drama. Instead of "I'm fine," you discover "I'm disappointed." Instead of "I'm stressed," you discover "I'm feeling trapped." This clarity reduces impulsive reactions and strengthens presence. It makes you easier to live with, not because you've become perfect, but because you've become clearer.

Clarity, Growth, and the Moment You Start to Return

As this practice continues, something changes in a quiet way. A person begins to regain focus—not because the phone is gone, and not because life has suddenly become easy, but because the inner world becomes less crowded. Writing clarifies priorities by revealing what keeps returning. It shows you what matters because it shows you what you cannot stop thinking about. It reveals where your attention is bleeding out and what your nervous system is trying to resolve.

This clarity leads to more intentional action. When people track their thoughts, patterns, and behaviors, follow-through increases. It's not because the journal is a motivational tool; it's because what gets written gets noticed, and what gets noticed can be improved. A person begins to recognize small choices that create large consequences. They begin to see where they are avoiding discomfort and where avoidance is costing them. Over time, they build self-trust—not the loud kind that comes from hype, but the quiet kind that comes from keeping a small promise to yourself each day.

Journaling also unlocks creativity and problem-solving. Many people get stuck in linear thinking: problem, panic, avoidance, repeat. Writing opens a different channel. It gives the mind room to wander without being hijacked by constant stimulation, and solutions often appear mid-sentence because the brain is finally allowed to explore. This is one reason creators, leaders, and high performers journal: it bypasses the inner critic and creates space for insight.

The deeper benefit arrives with time. A journal becomes a record of your humanity—your setbacks, your growth, your resilience, your confusion, and your courage. It helps you integrate hardship rather than letting hardship define you. Not by making pain "worth it," but by making experience usable, something you can learn from rather than something you must outrun. Over months, this practice can transform the way you relate to your own life. You begin to notice meaning where you previously only felt pressure, and wisdom where you previously only felt regret.

What the Wisest People Have Always Known

If journaling were a trend, it would have died long ago. It hasn't, because it works across personalities, cultures, and centuries. A psychologist who has spent decades studying expressive writing found that when people write honestly about emotional experiences for short periods of time, both mental and physical health improve. The mechanism is not mysterious: writing helps people organize emotional upheavals. Once structured, those experiences become more manageable.

Researchers who study vulnerability and shame have reached a similar conclusion from a different angle. Much of human suffering is intensified by what we refuse to name. When you write what you are afraid to say, you reduce the power it holds over you. You stop letting it remain a foggy threat and begin seeing it as something real—something you can address. Teachers of creativity have long argued that the value of daily writing is not in producing anything impressive, but in clearing mental clutter. The goal is honesty, not elegance. Consistency matters more than insight.

Psychiatrists who study the integration of the mind describe journaling as a way to create coherence—an internal order that improves emotional regulation. Entrepreneurs and high performers use journals to think clearly, reduce anxiety, and make high-leverage decisions. And long before modern research, a Roman emperor kept private reflections meant for no audience. Those pages were not performative; they were practice. They were an attempt to remain grounded, to correct himself, and to keep perspective in a chaotic world.

Across all these voices, the consensus is remarkably simple. Journaling works best when it is honest rather than performative, consistent rather than perfect, and private rather than polished. You do not journal to write well; you journal to think clearly and live intentionally.

This journal is designed for the real moment—the one that happens on the chair or couch at the end of the day, when you're tempted to disappear into stimulation because you feel empty, tense, or overloaded. If all you do is write a few true sentences, you are doing it correctly. Fifteen minutes can be enough to begin. Over time, many people notice something that feels almost like a quiet miracle: the urge to escape softens, the mind settles more easily, sleep improves, and a steady sense returns that you are back in charge of your attention and your life.

THE PRACTICE:
HOW TO CAPTURE THE DAY

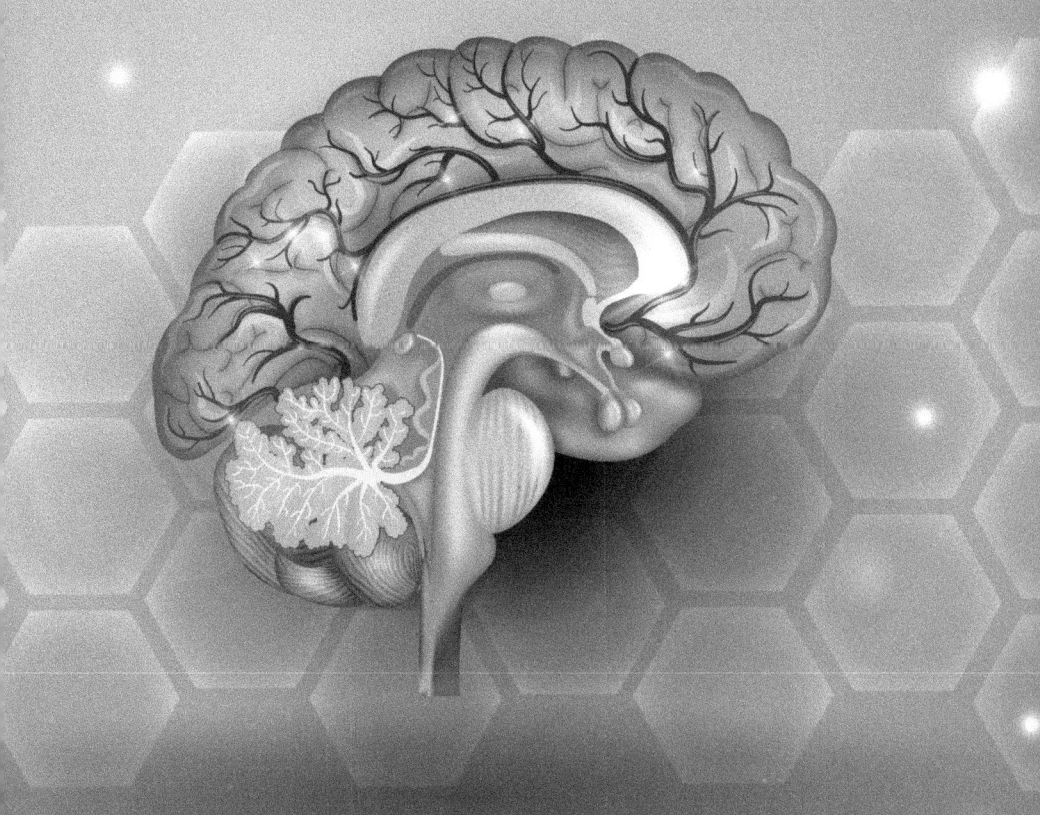

How to Use This Journal
(Or, How to Begin Without Getting It "Right")

Before anything else, it's important to say this clearly:

This is *your* journal.

It doesn't belong to a method, a philosophy, or an expectation. It doesn't need to sound a certain way or lead anywhere specific. Nothing in these pages will be graded, evaluated, or reviewed. No one else needs to see it. You don't need to justify it or explain it to anyone.

What follows is not a set of rules. It's guidance—meant to help you begin, especially on days when you're tired, distracted, or unsure what to write. If any of it helps, use it. If it doesn't, ignore it. The journal will still work.

The only thing that truly matters is that you start.

Most people hesitate at the beginning because they believe they need to do this well. They worry about saying the wrong thing, focusing on the wrong topic, or "wasting" a page. That hesitation is understandable, but it's also unnecessary. Journaling is not a performance. It's a practice. And like any practice, it gets easier—and more useful—over time.

Think of this journal less as a place to produce something and more as a place to put something down.

The simplest way to use it is this: write at the end of the day, or at the moment when you usually check out. Sit where you normally scroll. Set aside a short, defined window of time—fifteen minutes if you can, less if that's all you have—and write without stopping. You don't need to be calm. You don't need to be insightful. You don't even need to know what you're feeling. Start wherever you are.

If nothing comes to mind, write that. If what comes out feels repetitive, messy, or unimportant, keep going. Journals often sound boring before they become honest, and honest before they become useful. Trust that process. The value isn't in what you write on any given day, but in the act of returning.

You'll notice prompts at the top of each page. They are there to help you begin, not to limit you. You don't need to answer them directly or completely. You can treat them as an opening door and walk wherever you want from there. Some days you may write about events. Other days you may write about feelings, frustrations, worries, or things you never said out loud. All of that belongs here.

When you feel finished, stop. There's no need to reread what you wrote. This journal is not meant to be edited or refined. It's meant to be used. If you miss a day, or a week, or a month, nothing is broken. Simply return when you're ready. Progress in journaling is not measured by streaks or volume, but by willingness— the willingness to show up imperfectly and tell the truth as you understand it in that moment.

Over time, you may notice changes. You may begin to recognize patterns more quickly. You may feel less pressure at the end of the day. You may find that the urge to escape softens because you've already given your mind a place to unload. Or you may simply notice that you feel slightly more settled after writing than you did before. All of that counts.

This journal does not ask for perfection. It asks for presence.

If you write a few honest sentences, you're doing it right.

If you write badly, you're doing it right.

If you show up tired, distracted, or unsure, you're doing it right.

Start where you are. Let the practice meet you there.

You'll get better simply by continuing.

Turn the page when you're ready.

How to Use the Daily Pages
(One Spread at a Time)

The daily pages in this journal are intentionally simple. That simplicity is not an accident. It is part of what makes this work when you are tired.

At the end of the day, you don't need a complicated system. You need a doorway. You need a way to start. You need something that guides you without demanding too much.

Each time you open the journal, you'll use the same two-page spread:

On the **left page**, you unload what the day left inside you.
On the **right page**, you name what you need now.

That's it.

You don't need to fill the whole page. Some days you will. Many days you won't. This journal is not measured by volume. It is measured by relief. The goal is not to create impressive writing. The goal is to create space inside yourself.

Think of it like setting down a heavy bag you've been carrying all day. You don't need to describe the bag in perfect detail. You simply need to put it on the ground.

Here are a few ways to use the pages, depending on what kind of day you had:

If your day felt chaotic:
Write the facts first. What happened. What hit you. What you didn't expect. Often the emotion will appear once the events are named.

If your day felt emotionally heavy:
Write what you're feeling without explaining it. The point is not to justify your emotions, but to acknowledge them. The nervous system calms when it is allowed to tell the truth.

If your day felt numb or empty:

Write what you did, even if it seems boring. Write what you consumed. Write what you avoided. Numbness usually has a story underneath it, and writing often helps it surface gently.

If your mind won't stop looping:
Write the loop. Put it on the page exactly as it repeats. What stays inside the mind tends to multiply. What goes onto paper becomes finite.

If you don't know what to write:
Write that you don't know. That's not failure—it's honesty. And honesty is where this practice begins.

As you write, you may notice something subtle: your body participates. Your shoulders drop. Your breathing slows. Your jaw relaxes. The writing becomes less about "thinking" and more about releasing. This is why the journal works even when willpower doesn't. It doesn't ask you to force discipline. It gives the nervous system a safer way to complete the day.

When you feel finished, stop. Close the book. Let the day be done.

You can always return tomorrow.

The Two Prompts
(How This Journal Works)

This journal asks you the same two questions every day.

Not because your life is repetitive, and not because your days are all the same—but because when you're tired, what you need most is something you don't have to figure out. You need a doorway that opens without effort. You need a way to begin.

Most people don't avoid journaling because they dislike reflection. They avoid it because the blank page can feel like another demand. Another place you're supposed to be articulate, insightful, productive. And at the end of a long day, you don't need another performance. You need relief. You need a place where you can set down what you've been carrying without having to earn the right to rest.

That's what these two prompts are for.

The first one is simple:

1) What's Still With Me From Today?

This isn't asking you to recount your schedule or summarize your responsibilities. It's asking what remained unfinished inside you. What followed you home. What keeps replaying even though the day is over. It's the sharp edge of a conversation you can't quite let go of, the pressure you swallowed so you could keep going, the quiet disappointment you didn't admit, the tension in your body that doesn't have a name yet.

Most people don't scroll because their lives are easy. They scroll because something inside them is still awake—still braced, still working, still holding the day together. This question gently invites that unfinished weight out of the dark and onto the page, where it becomes something you can see, and therefore something you don't have to keep carrying alone.

The second prompt follows it:

2) Right Now, What I Need Most Is...

This is where the journal stops being a place to unload and becomes a place to recover.

Sometimes what you need will be practical: sleep, water, food, quiet, a plan for tomorrow. Sometimes it will be emotional: reassurance, room to breathe, permission to be imperfect, forgiveness, connection, a little hope. And sometimes it will be so honest it surprises you—something you've been trying not to admit, like: *I need to stop pretending this doesn't hurt.*

This question isn't about fixing your life in one sitting. It's about telling the truth in a small way that your nervous system can feel. It's about giving yourself the one thing the world rarely gives you: a moment of care that is not earned, negotiated, or performed—only received.

Together, these two questions do something quietly powerful. They help you complete the day.

You don't have to solve everything. You don't have to reach clarity on every problem. You only have to give the day a place to land, so it doesn't have to keep moving through you all night.

And that is how people begin to come back—one page at a time.

15-Minute Reset
(A Simple Daily Practice)

You do not need an hour.

You do not need perfect conditions.

You do not need a quiet mind, a clean house, or the kind of life where evenings are calm and predictable.

You only need a small window of time—small enough that you can actually do it, even when you are worn down. Fifteen minutes is not a magic number. It's simply a bridge: long enough to change the way the day feels inside you, short enough that you don't resist starting.

This is the practice.

Find the place where you normally disappear. The chair, the couch, the corner of the bed. Sit in the exact spot where your hand would usually reach for the screen. This journal is meant to live in the same territory as your habits, because the goal isn't to become a different person in a different life—it's to change one moment in the life you already have.

Open the journal.

Don't wait to feel ready. Ready is rare. Begin anyway.

Start on the left page:

1. What's Still With Me From Today?
Write what comes. It can be messy. It can be repetitive. It can be plain and un-impressive. You are not writing to sound wise—you are writing to stop carrying what has been lodged inside you since morning. Let the page take it.

If you don't know where to start, begin with a sentence that tells the truth:

I can't stop thinking about...
What bothered me today was...
What I didn't say was...
I'm more tired than I expected because...

Then move to the right page:

2. Right Now, What I Need Most Is...

This is the turning point—the moment you stop treating yourself like a machine that should keep going and start treating yourself like a human being who needs care.

You may already know the answer. Or you may feel blank. Either is fine. If the words don't come easily, try finishing a simple sentence:

I would feel better if I...
What I need tonight is...
My nervous system needs...
Tomorrow will go better if I...

Then stop when something shifts. Not when everything is solved—just when the pressure is lower than it was.

That shift matters more than the amount you wrote.

Fifteen minutes is enough to change your relationship with the night. Enough to bring you back into your own life before the evening disappears. Enough to end the day with yourself instead of ending it with the world.

And if you still choose to check your phone afterward, you can.

But now it's a choice—not an escape.

When You Miss a Day
(How to Restart Without Shame)

You will miss days.

Not because you are inconsistent. Not because you didn't want this badly enough. Simply because you are a person living a real life, and real lives are full of noise, fatigue, and seasons where even good things feel hard to reach for.

Often, the days you need this journal most will be the days you feel least capable of using it.

When you are overloaded, the nervous system does not crave growth. It craves relief. It reaches for what is immediate, familiar, and effortless. That is not failure. That is biology. That is the body trying to protect you in the only way it knows.

This is why the journal cannot be a streak.

A streak turns a practice into a test. It makes the whole thing fragile. Miss one day and the mind begins its old song: *See? You never follow through. You always quit.*

This journal is not here to give shame another place to live.

It is here to give you a way back.

So if you miss a day—or a week—or a month—do not catch up. Do not punish yourself. Do not try to rewrite yesterday. Just open to the next blank page and begin again, exactly where you are.

You can start small.

Three sentences. One sentence. A single honest line.

You can even write something as plain as:

I don't want to do this tonight, but I'm here.

That counts. More than you think.

Because the goal is not perfection. The goal is return.

The goal is to build an off-ramp that stays available to you, especially on the nights when escape is calling the loudest. And the more often you return—even clumsily, even briefly—the more natural it becomes.

When you miss a day, you don't lose progress. You simply pause the practice.

And you can restart in less than a minute.

Open the journal.

Tell the truth.

Let the day land somewhere other than your body.

The journal will meet you here, every time.

Turn the page when you're ready.

JOURNAL PAGES

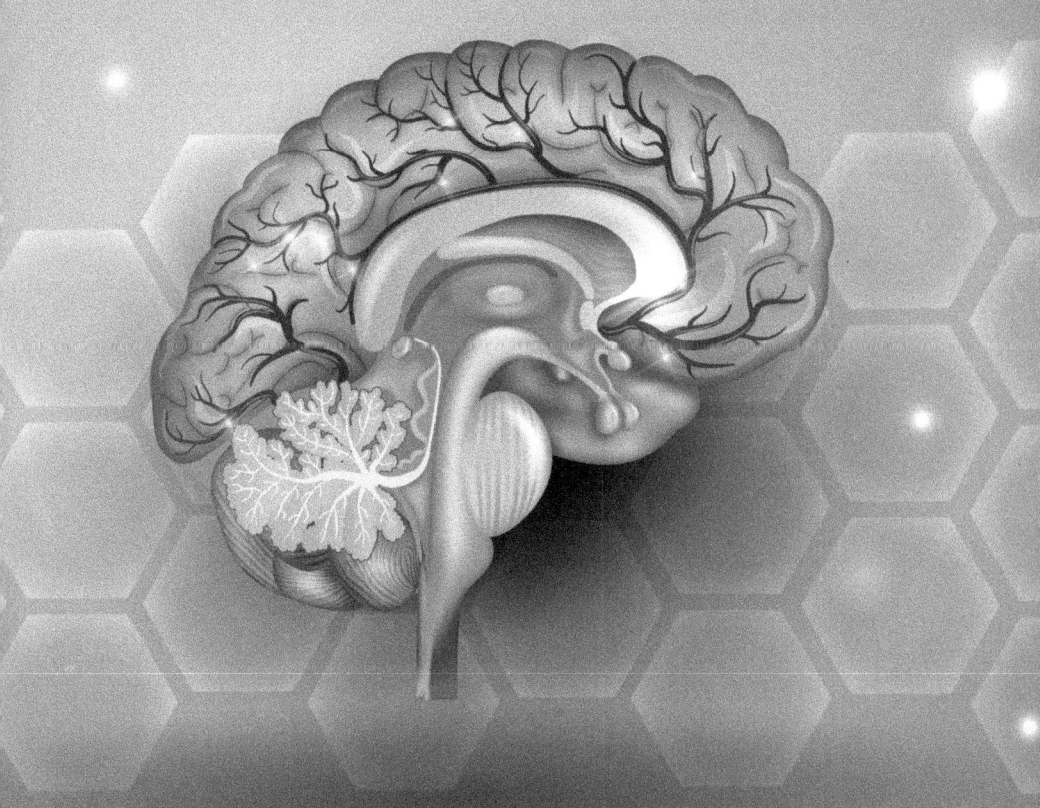

Left Page Supporting Questions

Main Prompt: What's Still With Me From Today?
Use any of these as your entry point:

- *What happened today that I haven't fully processed yet?*
- *What moment keeps replaying in my head?*
- *What am I still carrying from a conversation, decision, or situation?*
- *What felt unresolved or incomplete?*
- *What frustrated me more than it should have?*
- *What drained me today?*
- *What surprised me today (good or bad)?*
- *What did I keep pushing down just to get through the day?*
- *What emotion followed me around today?*
- *What did I need today but didn't get?*
- *What did I tolerate that I shouldn't keep tolerating?*
- *Where did I feel tension in my body today, and why?*
- *What did I avoid today?*
- *What did I do today that I'm proud of—even if it was small?*
- *What am I worried about tonight?*
- *What's the truth about today that I haven't admitted yet?*
- *What did I do well today, even under pressure?*
- *What am I still trying to "solve" in my mind?*
- *What would I like to put down before I go to sleep?*
- *If today had a headline, what would it be?*

Right Page Supporting Questions

Main Prompt: Right Now, What I Need Most Is...

Use these to shift from overload to clarity:

- *What would help me feel 10% better right now?*
- *What do I need emotionally that I'm not giving myself?*
- *What do I need physically right now? (Sleep, water, food, movement)*
- *What do I need to stop doing tonight?*
- *What do I need to forgive myself for today?*
- *What do I need to hear right now?*
- *What would "support" look like for me tonight?*
- *What boundary do I need to hold or rebuild?*
- *What am I asking my phone to do for me right now?*
- *What is the healthy substitute for that?*
- *What is one small thing I can do that would help tomorrow?*
- *What can wait until tomorrow—and still be okay?*
- *What decision do I not need to make tonight?*
- *What does my nervous system need right now: quiet, movement, connection, or space?*
- *What would I do tonight if I believed I mattered?*
- *What would it look like to end the day with respect for myself?*
- *What's one simple win I can give myself before bed?*
- *What do I need to let go of control over?*
- *What's the next right step—not the whole plan?*
- *If I could give myself one thing tonight, what would it be?*

Date _____

What's Still With Me From Today?

Date _____

Right Now, What I Need Most Is...

Date _____

What's Still With Me From Today?

Date _____

Right Now, What I Need Most Is...

Date _____

What's Still With Me From Today?

Date _____

Right Now, What I Need Most Is...

Date _____

What's Still With Me From Today?

Right Now, What I Need Most Is...

Date _____

What's Still With Me From Today?

Date _____

Right Now, What I Need Most Is...

Date _____

What's Still With Me From Today?

Date _____

Right Now, What I Need Most Is...

Date _____

What's Still With Me From Today?

Right Now, What I Need Most Is...

Date _____

What's Still With Me From Today?

Date _____

Right Now, What I Need Most Is...

Date _____

What's Still With Me From Today?

Right Now, What I Need Most Is...

Date _____

What's Still With Me From Today?

Date _____

Right Now, What I Need Most Is...

Date _____

What's Still With Me From Today?

Date _____

Right Now, What I Need Most Is...

Date _____

What's Still With Me From Today?

Right Now, What I Need Most Is...

Date _____

What's Still With Me From Today?

Right Now, What I Need Most Is...

Date _____

What's Still With Me From Today?

Date _____

Right Now, What I Need Most Is...

Date _____

What's Still With Me From Today?

Right Now, What I Need Most Is...

Date _____

What's Still With Me From Today?

Right Now, What I Need Most Is...

Date _____

What's Still With Me From Today?

Date _____

Right Now, What I Need Most Is...

Date _____

What's Still With Me From Today?

Date _____

Right Now, What I Need Most Is...

Date _____

What's Still With Me From Today?

Right Now, What I Need Most Is...

Date _____

What's Still With Me From Today?

Date _____

Right Now, What I Need Most Is...

Date _____

What's Still With Me From Today?

Date _____

Right Now, What I Need Most Is...

Date _____

What's Still With Me From Today?

Date _____

Right Now, What I Need Most Is...

Date _____

What's Still With Me From Today?

Date _____

Right Now, What I Need Most Is...

Date _____

What's Still With Me From Today?

Date _____

Right Now, What I Need Most Is...

Date _____

What's Still With Me From Today?

Right Now, What I Need Most Is...

Date _____

What's Still With Me From Today?

Right Now, What I Need Most Is...

Date _____

What's Still With Me From Today?

Right Now, What I Need Most Is...

Date _____

What's Still With Me From Today?

Right Now, What I Need Most Is...

Date _____

What's Still With Me From Today?

Date _____

Right Now, What I Need Most Is...

Date _____

What's Still With Me From Today?

Date _____

Right Now, What I Need Most Is...

Date _____

What's Still With Me From Today?

Date _____

Right Now, What I Need Most Is...

Date _____

What's Still With Me From Today?

Date _____

Right Now, What I Need Most Is...

Date _____

What's Still With Me From Today?

Right Now, What I Need Most Is...

Date _____

What's Still With Me From Today?

Date _____

Right Now, What I Need Most Is...

Date _____

What's Still With Me From Today?

Right Now, What I Need Most Is...

Date _____

What's Still With Me From Today?

Date _____

Right Now, What I Need Most Is...

Date _____

What's Still With Me From Today?

Date _____

Right Now, What I Need Most Is...

Date _____

What's Still With Me From Today?

Right Now, What I Need Most Is...

Date _____

What's Still With Me From Today?

Right Now, What I Need Most Is...

Date _____

What's Still With Me From Today?

Date _____

Right Now, What I Need Most Is...

Date _____

What's Still With Me From Today?

Right Now, What I Need Most Is...

Date _____

What's Still With Me From Today?

Right Now, What I Need Most Is...

Date _____

What's Still With Me From Today?

Right Now, What I Need Most Is...

Date _____

What's Still With Me From Today?

Right Now, What I Need Most Is...

Date _____

What's Still With Me From Today?

Right Now, What I Need Most Is...

Date _____

What's Still With Me From Today?

Date _____

Right Now, What I Need Most Is...

Date _____

What's Still With Me From Today?

Date _____

Right Now, What I Need Most Is...

Date _____

What's Still With Me From Today?

Right Now, What I Need Most Is...

Date _____

What's Still With Me From Today?

Right Now, What I Need Most Is...

Date _____

What's Still With Me From Today?

Right Now, What I Need Most Is...

Date _____

What's Still With Me From Today?

Date _____

Right Now, What I Need Most Is...

Date _____

What's Still With Me From Today?

Right Now, What I Need Most Is...

Date _____

What's Still With Me From Today?

Right Now, What I Need Most Is...

Date _____

What's Still With Me From Today?

Right Now, What I Need Most Is...

Date _____

What's Still With Me From Today?

Right Now, What I Need Most Is...

Date _____

What's Still With Me From Today?

Date _____

Right Now, What I Need Most Is...

Date _____

What's Still With Me From Today?

Date _____

Right Now, What I Need Most Is...

Date _____

What's Still With Me From Today?

Date _____

Right Now, What I Need Most Is...

Date _____

What's Still With Me From Today?

Right Now, What I Need Most Is...

Date _____

What's Still With Me From Today?

Date _____

Right Now, What I Need Most Is...

Date _____

What's Still With Me From Today?

Date _____

Right Now, What I Need Most Is...

Date _____

What's Still With Me From Today?

Date _____

Right Now, What I Need Most Is...

Date _____

What's Still With Me From Today?

Right Now, What I Need Most Is...

Date _____

What's Still With Me From Today?

Date _____

Right Now, What I Need Most Is...

Date _____

What's Still With Me From Today?

Date _____

Right Now, What I Need Most Is...

Date _____

What's Still With Me From Today?

Date _____

Right Now, What I Need Most Is...

Date _____

What's Still With Me From Today?

Right Now, What I Need Most Is...

Date _____

What's Still With Me From Today?

Right Now, What I Need Most Is...

Date _____

What's Still With Me From Today?

Date _____

Right Now, What I Need Most Is...

Date _____

What's Still With Me From Today?

Right Now, What I Need Most Is...

Date _____

What's Still With Me From Today?

Date _____

Right Now, What I Need Most Is...

Date _____

What's Still With Me From Today?

Right Now, What I Need Most Is...

Date _____

What's Still With Me From Today?

Right Now, What I Need Most Is...

Date _____

What's Still With Me From Today?

Date _____

Right Now, What I Need Most Is...

Date _____

What's Still With Me From Today?

Right Now, What I Need Most Is...

Date _____

What's Still With Me From Today?

Date _____

Right Now, What I Need Most Is...

Date _____

What's Still With Me From Today?

Date _____

Right Now, What I Need Most Is...

Date _____

What's Still With Me From Today?

Date _____

Right Now, What I Need Most Is...

Date _____

What's Still With Me From Today?

Date _____

Right Now, What I Need Most Is...

Date _____

What's Still With Me From Today?

Date _____

Right Now, What I Need Most Is...

Date _____

What's Still With Me From Today?

Date _____

Right Now, What I Need Most Is...

Date _____

What's Still With Me From Today?

Date _____

Right Now, What I Need Most Is...

Date _____

What's Still With Me From Today?

Right Now, What I Need Most Is...

Date _____

What's Still With Me From Today?

Right Now, What I Need Most Is...

CLOSING

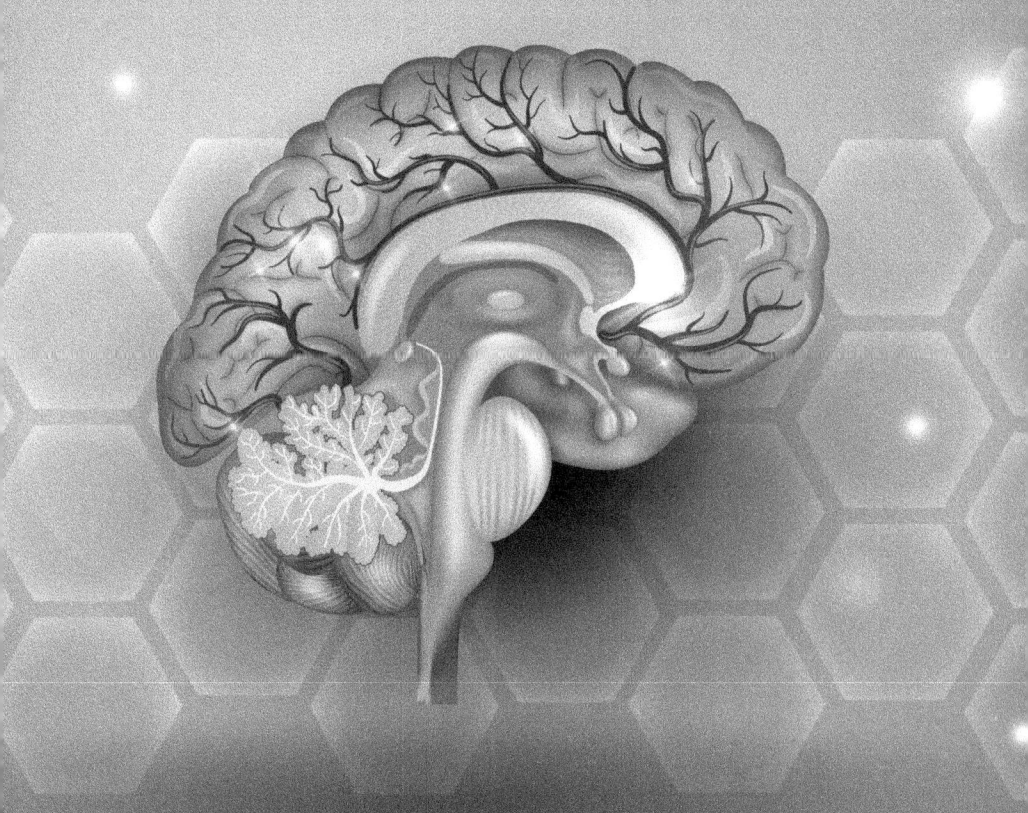

Reflections

You've reached the end of these pages.

That doesn't mean the work is finished, and it doesn't mean you've "arrived." It simply means you stayed with it long enough to place a stretch of your life somewhere honest. And that matters more than most people realize.

Many journals end abruptly, as if the writing itself is the only point. But this journal was never meant to be a record. It was meant to be a release. A place where the day could land so it wouldn't keep following you into the night.

If you used this journal even occasionally, you may have noticed something—maybe not dramatic, but real. A small loosening. A quieter mind. A little more space inside your body. A return to yourself that didn't require escaping first.

These changes rarely announce themselves. They arrive quietly, and they grow slowly. But they are worth noticing, because the kind of progress that restores a life is often the kind that looks small from the outside.

This section exists for one reason: to help you see what your own pages have already been showing you.

Not so you can evaluate yourself.

Not so you can judge your effort.

But so you can recognize what has been shifting beneath the surface.

Take a few minutes, if you want. Read a page or two from earlier in the journal, or simply reflect from memory. Let this be a closing moment—an exhale at the end of a season.

Then write whatever is true.

Looking Back

What changed in me while I used this journal?

_____

_____

What did I start to notice about my evenings?

_____

_____

What patterns kept returning—thoughts, emotions, situations, triggers?

_____

_____

When I wanted to disappear, what was I really trying to escape?

_____

_____

What did I seem to need most when I was tired?

_____

_____

What helped me feel more present—even slightly?

_____

_____

What do I want to keep doing, because it worked?

_____

_____

What do I want to stop doing, because it costs too much?

_____

_____

What would I tell my future self to remember?

_____

_____

One Last Question

Right now, what I need most is...

_____

_____

Last Page

If you've made it to the end of this journal, you've done something rare—you chose presence over escape, long enough to start taking your attention back. If these pages helped you, I have one small request: please leave a brief review on Amazon so this journal can reach the people who are still searching for a way to put the day down instead of carrying it into the night.

Scan here to leave a review on Amazon:

Bring This Conversation to Your Organization

The ideas in this journal come alive when leaders experience them together.

I work with organizations that want less drama, clearer communication, and leadership that actually works in the real world. If you're looking for a speaker who connects deeply, challenges thinking, and leaves people changed—not just motivated—I'd love to continue the conversation.

Scan here to learn more about booking Jim Koetting to speak:

www.ingramcontent.com/pod-product-compliance
Lightning Source LLC
Chambersburg PA
CBHW051516120626
46551CB00012B/943